M000049804

This journal belongs to

_____

MY
BEACH
JOURNAL

"Come away and rest a while."
MARK 6:31 NRSV

Belle City Gifts
Racine, Wisconsin, USA

Belle City Gifts is an imprint of BroadStreet Publishing Group LLC.
Broadstreetpublishing.com

Come Away and Rest

© 2017 BroadStreet Publishing

ISBN 978-1-4245-5487-4

All rights reserved. No part of this publication may be reproduced, distributed, or transmitted
in any form or by any means, including photocopying, recording, or other electronic or
mechanical methods, without the prior written permission of the publisher, except in the
case of brief quotations embodied in critical reviews and certain other noncommercial uses
permitted by copyright law.

Scripture quotations marked (NLT) are taken from the Holy Bible, New Living Translation,
copyright © 1996, 2004, 2007. Used by permission of Tyndale House Publishers, Inc., Carol
Stream, Illinois 60188. All rights reserved. Scripture quotations marked (NIV) are taken from
the Holy Bible, New International Version®, NIV®. Copyright © 1973, 1978, 1984, 2011
by Biblica, Inc.™ Used by permission of Zondervan. All rights reserved worldwide. www.
zondervan.com. The "NIV" and "New International Version" are trademarks registered in
the United States Patent and Trademark Office by Biblica, Inc.™ Scripture quotations marked
(NCV) are taken from the New Century Version®. Copyright © 2005 by Thomas Nelson.
Used by permission. All rights reserved. Scripture quotations marked (AMP) are taken from
the Amplified Bible, Copyright © 1954, 1958, 1962, 1964, 1965, 1987 by The Lockman
Foundation. Used by permission. Scripture quotations marked (NASB) are taken from the
New American Standard Bible®, Copyright © 1960, 1962, 1963, 1968, 1971, 1972, 1973,
1975, 1977, 1995 by The Lockman Foundation. Used by permission. www.Lockman.org.
Scripture quotations marked (NRSV) are taken from the New Revised Standard Version
Bible, copyright 1989, Division of Christian Education of the National Council of the Churches
of Christ in the United States of America. Used by permission. All rights reserved. Scripture
quotations marked (ESV) are from the ESV® Bible (The Holy Bible, English Standard
Version®), copyright © 2001 by Crossway, a publishing ministry of Good News Publishers.
Used by permission. All rights reserved. Scripture quotations marked (TLB) are taken from
The Living Bible copyright © 1971. Used by permission of Tyndale House Publishers, Inc.,
Carol Stream, Illinois 60188. All rights reserved. Scripture quotations marked (NKJV) are
taken from the New King James Version®. Copyright © 1982 by Thomas Nelson. Used
by permission. All rights reserved. Scripture quotations marked (TPT) are taken from The
Passion Translation® of the Holy Bible. Copyright © 2014, 2015 by BroadStreet Publishing.
All rights reserved.

Design by Garborg Design Works | garborgdesign.com
Compiled and edited by Michelle Winger | literallyprecise.com

Printed in China.

17   18   19   20   21   22   23   7   6   5   4   3   2   1

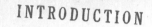

INTRODUCTION

If there is one thing that a woman can appreciate, it's something pretty. Shiny things easily catch our attention, and we seek to surround ourselves with beauty. There is nothing wrong with finding loveliness in our world, but if there is one thing that is more beautiful than anything else, it is God himself. His love, his mercy, his grace, and his understanding— it is nothing short of breathtaking.

You've been created to enjoy all that is exquisite, beautiful, and captivating. Give in to that desire, and find it in him! Don't miss the beauty of God today. Seek it, and you will find it. Rest in his perfect love and be refreshed.

Commit your actions to the LORD,
and your plans will succeed.

PROVERBS 16:3 NLT

You don't have to be willing *and* able;
you can just be willing because *God* is able.

May he give you the power to accomplish all the good things
your faith prompts you to do.

2 THESSALONIANS 1:11 NLT

Let your thoughts stretch above the canopy of everyday
human details to bask in this joy: God has given you
everything you need in Jesus.

He has saved us and called us to a holy life—
not because of anything we have done
but because of his own purpose and grace.

2 TIMOTHY 1:9 NIV

When we've given up, run away, lost the plot, or stumbled and fallen,
God doesn't give up on us.

I will praise You,
for I am fearfully and wonderfully made;
Marvelous are Your works,
And that my soul knows very well.

PSALM 139:4 NKJV

God's Word says that he makes all things beautiful in his time.
All things. Whatever situation you are facing right now
has the potential to create beauty in you.

"Until now you have not asked for anything in my name.
Ask and you will receive, and your joy will be complete."

JOHN 16:24 NIV

Joy flows in the middle of the darkness as we trust in God's perfect ways.

It is God who makes us able to do all that we do.

2 CORINTHIANS 12:9 ESV

When we allow ourselves to be weak,
we give God the opportunity to show his strength—
and he'll take that opportunity every time we give it to him.

Long ago, even before he made the world,
God chose us to be his very own through what Christ
would do for us; he decided then to make us holy in his eyes,
without a single fault—we who stand before him covered with his love.

EPHESIANS 1:4 TLB

With God, our acceptance has already been promised.

"I know that my Redeemer lives,
and he will stand upon the earth at last."

JOB 19:25-27 NLT

Everything on earth is a fleeting treasure, a momentary comfort
that can be lost in a flash. But the assurance of your
eternal place in his kingdom is indestructible.

His divine power has given us everything we need
for a godly life through our knowledge of him
who called us by his own glory and goodness.

2 PETER 1:3 NIV

God is real, and he is good. He has given us an example of how to remain authentic in a world full of fraud and deception.

Let us come boldly to the throne of our gracious God. There we will receive his mercy, and we will find grace to help us when we need it most.

HEBREWS 4:16 NLT

Approach the throne, and shamelessly pull up a chair.
God loves your company.

To all who mourn... he will give: beauty for ashes;
joy instead of mourning; praise instead of heaviness.
For God has planted them like strong
and graceful oaks for his own glory.

ISAIAH 61:3 TLB

You are not a weak sapling, limited by inadequate light
and meager nourishment. You are a strong and graceful oak,
soaring and resilient for the glory of God.

The Lord is compassionate and gracious,
Slow to anger and abounding in lovingkindness.

PSALM 103:8 NASB

We aren't dealt with as we deserve; rather, according
to God's great love for us. Can we say the same
about how we treat others?

When you go through deep waters and great trouble,
I will be with you. When you go through rivers of difficulty,
you will not drown! When you walk through the fire of oppression,
you will not be burned up—the flames will not consume you.

ISAIAH 43:2 TLB

Let no doubt take root; God is a God who cares deeply, loves fully,
and remains faithful, ever at our side in times of trouble.

Sketch or attach a photo of a favorite day at the beach.

You, O LORD, are a shield about me,
My glory, and the One who lifts my head.

PSALM 3:3 NASB

Life is full of painful moments that creep up unexpectedly,
but it's also full of second chances. Don't give up.

I can do all this through him
who gives me strength.

PHILIPPIANS 4:12-13 NIV

The season of your greatest rejoicing can be now,
when you consider the strength God provides.

I eagerly expect and hope that I will in no way be ashamed,
but will have sufficient courage so that now as always Christ
will be exalted in my body, whether by life or by death.

PHILIPPIANS 1:20 NIV

Having courage, being brave, remaining firm—we can only hold on for so long. Sometimes we need to recognize that it's time to call on the supernatural strength of our Father in heaven.

I waited patiently for the LORD;
he turned to me and heard my cry.
He lifted me out of the slimy pit,
out of the mud and mire;
he set my feet on a rock
and gave me a firm place to stand.

PSALM 40:1-2 NIV

God loves us with a sacrificial love that escapes our human understanding,
overwhelms our human selfishness, and humbles our human pride.

He put a new song in my mouth,
a hymn of praise to our God.
Many will see and fear the LORD
and put their trust in him.

PSALM 40:3 NIV

God has done the impossible task of making us into something worthy;
he takes us from instability to security, gives us a song of praise,
and makes our conversion a testimony for all creation to see.

I will sing of the LORD's great love forever;
with my mouth I will make your faithfulness known
through all generations.
I will declare that your love stands firm forever,
that you have established your faithfulness in heaven itself.

PSALM 89:1-2 NIV

This truth is overwhelmingly satisfying; when such devotion has been proven, what else could attract our gaze?

The humble will see their God at work and be glad.
Let all who seek God's help be encouraged.

PSALM 69:32 NLT

Ever encouraging, our God beckons us:
Come to me. You can make it. You're almost there.

He has made everything beautiful in its time.
He has also set eternity in the human heart;
yet no one can fathom what God has done
from beginning to end.

ECCLESIASTES 3:11 NIV

Time gives us better perspective on the true definition of beauty.
Spending time with those we love affords us a glimpse
into the depth of beauty that lies within.

He will wipe away every tear from their eyes, and death shall be no more,
neither shall there be mourning, nor crying, nor pain anymore,
for the former things have passed away.

REVELATION 21:4 ESV

All things become bearable and light under the assurance of seeing Jesus, embracing him, and gazing on his beauty!

Through Christ you have come to trust in God.
And you have placed your faith and hope in God because
he raised Christ from the dead and gave him great glory.

1 PETER 1:21 NLT

As we leap, sometimes stumbling, along the cliffs of life, who can we trust? Only Jesus—the rock that will not fail, will not crumble, and will never falter under our weight.

Your lovingkindness, O Lord, extends to the heavens,
Your faithfulness reaches to the skies.

PSALM 36:5 NASB

The price Jesus paid to restore our relationship with God
was his life. He gave up everything to bring us home.
That is faithfulness in its fullest measure.

When you lie down, you will not be afraid;
Yes, you will lie down and your sleep will be sweet.
Do not be afraid of sudden terror,
Nor of trouble from the wicked when it comes;
For the Lord will be your confidence.

PROVERBS 3:24-26 NKJV

If we can learn to fully trust God, he will calm our fears
and still our quickened hearts.

Sketch or attach a photo of a favorite day at the beach.

Creation itself will be set free from its bondage to corruption and obtain the freedom of the glory of the children of God.

ROMANS 8:21 ESV

When you spend time with God, there is no need to hide.
You can be exactly who you are. You can say everything
you want to say. There is freedom in his presence.

"Here I am! I stand at the door and knock.
If anyone hears my voice and opens the door,
I will come in and eat with that person, and they with me."

REVELATION 3:20 NIV

Train your heart to run first to God with your pain, joy, frustration, and excitement. His friendship will never let you down!

He gives more grace. Therefore He says:
"God resists the proud,
But gives grace to the humble."

JAMES 4:6 NKJV

God's only requirement for ample grace is humility.
When we stop thinking we can get through life just fine on our own,
he stands ready with his grace.

All the paths of the LORD are steadfast love and faithfulness,
for those who keep his covenant and his testimonies.

PSALM 25:10 ESV

Your path has been chosen and your feet have been set upon it.
Truly, it is a path of love and faithfulness.

> "Daughter, your faith has made you well;
> go in peace and be healed of your affliction."

MARK 5:34 NASB

Often, we become fixated on doctoring our own wounds so we can make it through the day. Why not turn instead to the one who can fully repair us?

There is surely a future hope for you,
and your hope will not be cut off.

PROVERBS 23:18 NIV

Hope starts with the promises of God.

The precepts of the LORD are right,
giving joy to the heart.
The commands of the LORD are radiant,
giving light to the eyes.

PSALM 19:8 NIV

Described as right and radiant, God's loving instructions keep us safe.
They draw us nearer to our Father and give joy and light.

Lord, you know everything there is to know about me.
You've examined my innermost being
With your loving gaze.

PSALM 139:1 TPT

God doesn't take a stab in the dark when you are approaching him, guessing a name and hoping he gets it right. He knows exactly who you are and why you are coming to him.

Be truly glad. There is wonderful joy ahead.
You love him even though you have never seen him.
Though you do not see him now, you trust him;
and you rejoice with a glorious, inexpressible joy.

1 PETER 1:6, 8 NLT

The purest form of joy is often experienced in the arms of sorrow.

He did not retaliate when he was insulted,
nor threaten revenge when he suffered.
He left his case in the hands of God,
who always judges fairly.

1 PETER 2:23 NLT

We don't leave our judgment in the hands of a jury. Even the most expensive defense attorney can't make a case against us that will last into eternity. God knows what happened, and, more importantly, he knows our hearts.

The LORD directs the steps of the godly.
He delights in every detail of their lives.
Though they stumble, they will never fall,
for the LORD holds them by the hand.

PSALM 37:23-24 NLT

We cannot fall when we follow God's lead
because his loving grip will never let us go.

"I am the resurrection and the life. He who believes in me, though he may die, he shall live."

JOHN 11:25 NKJV

For those who don't have salvation in Jesus Christ,
this side of life has the greatest happiness they will ever experience;
for followers of God, it has the least.

We love because he first loved us. If anyone says, "I love God,"
and hates his brother, he is a liar; for he who does not love his brother
whom he has seen cannot love God whom he has not seen.

1 JOHN 4:19-20 ESV

We love to the degree that we understand his love for us.

Happy are those
who do not follow the advice of the wicked,
or take the path that sinners tread,
or sit in the seat of scoffers;
but their delight is in the law of the Lord,
and on his law they meditate day and night.

PSALM 1:1-2 NRSV

Thanks to a modern diet of technology and social media,
women today can feast on heaping portions of gossip, envy, boastful pride,
and selfishness. It is not a nourishing diet, but it is deviously sweet.
Delight yourself in God's Word and be truly refreshed.

Sketch or attach a photo of a
favorite day at the beach.

"Peace I leave with you; my peace I give you. I do not give to you as the world gives. Do not let your hearts be troubled and do not be afraid."

JOHN 14:27 NIV

The peace begged for on bumper stickers will always elude the world;
the peace of God is the only lasting peace, the only true peace
that we can attain while walking this earth.

Let us throw off everything that hinders and the sin
that so easily entangles. And let us run with perseverance
the race marked out for us, fixing our eyes on Jesus...
so that you will not grow weary and lose heart.

HEBREWS 12:1-3 NIV

You might run. You might crawl. You might move mere inches per day.
But if you remove the tangles of sin and keep your eyes fixed on him,
you won't grow weary and lose heart.

Why am I praying like this? Because I know you will answer me, O God!
Yes, listen as I pray.

PSALM 17:6 TLB

Not only does God *hear* your prayers when they tumble clumsily
from your lips, he knows what you need prior to you asking.

Let all who take refuge in you be glad;
let them ever sing for joy.
Spread your protection over them,
that those who love your name may rejoice in you.

PSALM 5:11 NIV

Imagine delighting through a storm, singing while structures
come crashing down, knowing all the while that you were standing
under the mighty hand of God.

Because of our faith, Christ has brought us into this place of undeserved privilege where we now stand, and we confidently and joyfully look forward to sharing God's glory.

ROMANS 5:2 NLT

As if eternity in his kingdom weren't enough,
God blesses us each and every day,
whether we acknowledge it or not.

Teach me your ways, O LORD,
that I may live according to your truth!
Grant me purity of heart,
so that I may honor you.

PSALM 86:11 NLT

Finding and ridding ourselves of all impurity can be a slow and painful process.
The good news is we don't have to try to purify ourselves.
We allow God to do it for us.

The LORD will fulfill his purpose for me;
your steadfast love, O LORD, endures forever.
Do not forsake the work of your hands.

PSALM 138:8 ESV

Hardships provide a distinct opportunity for God
to mold us more into his image.

"The water I give them," he said, "becomes a perpetual spring within them, watering them forever with eternal life."

JOHN 4:13-14 TLB

God's Word will never run dry. It is life-giving and eternal! The *perpetual spring* is in you, ready to be drawn upon at any moment of the day.

"So everyone, come to me! Are you weary, carrying a heavy burden?
Then come to me. I will refresh your life, for I am your oasis."

MATTHEW 11:28 TPT

Accepting that we need help can sometimes be the hardest part.
Once we let go of the need to appear as if everything is ok,
we are in a better position to receive help.

Bless the LORD, O my soul,
and forget not all his benefits.
Who satisfies you with good
so that your youth is renewed like the eagle's.

PSALM 103:2, 5 ESV

Whether you are at peak performance or running on empty, needing renewal now or in the future, God alone can give you what you need.

"I will make darkness light before them,
And crooked places straight.
These things I will do for them,
And not forsake them."

ISAIAH 42:16 NKJV

Breathe in this fresh start: today is a new day, full of promise and life.

Wherever I am, though far away at the ends of the earth,
I will cry to you for help. When my heart is faint
and overwhelmed, lead me to the mighty,
towering Rock of safety. For you are my refuge,
a high tower where my enemies can never reach me.

PSALM 61:2-3 TLB

God loves you with a fiercely protective, eternally faithful, inescapable love.

In peace I will lie down and sleep,
for you alone, LORD,
make me dwell in safety.

PSALM 4:8 NIV

Don't look anywhere else for your security. Find it in God.

Do not be anxious about anything, but in every situation,
by prayer and petition, with thanksgiving, present your
requests to God. And the peace of God, which transcends
all understanding, will guard your hearts and your minds in Christ Jesus.

PHILIPPIANS 4:6-7 NIV

It may seem difficult to give thanks in the midst of trouble and fear, but when we do, God replaces our worries with peace.

Sketch or attach a photo of a
favorite day at the beach.

Let your roots grow down into him, and let your lives be built on him.
Then your faith will grow strong in the truth you were taught,
and you will overflow with thankfulness.

COLOSSIANS 2:7 NLT

Build on the rock and your house will not fall.

Whom have I in heaven but you?
And earth has nothing I desire besides you.
My flesh and my heart may fail,
but God is the strength of my heart
and my portion forever.

PSALM 73:25-26 NIV

When the world around you seems to have collapsed, and you find yourself floundering around looking for something firm to take hold of, grab God's hand. He is steady and sure, and his love is safe.

I fall to my knees and pray to the Father, the Creator of everything in heaven and on earth. I pray that from his glorious, unlimited resources he will empower you with inner strength through his Spirit.

EPHESIANS 3:14 NLT

Pray until the life and power of God break through the clouds
and shine brightly upon your face. He is all you need.

Send out your light and your truth;
let them lead me;
let them bring me to your holy hill
and to your dwelling.

PSALM 43:3 NRSV

Our best line of defense is to surround ourselves with the truth.
Read it. Think it. Pray it. Declare it.

"My sheep hear my voice, and I know them, and they follow me.
I give them eternal life, and they will never perish,
and no one will snatch them out of my hand."

JOHN 10:27-28 ESV

We need to listen for the quiet, familiar voice of our Shepherd,
so we will know which way to turn for safety.

Can anything ever separate us from Christ's love?
No, despite all these things, overwhelming victory is ours
through Christ, who loved us.

ROMANS 8:35, 37 NLT

It's tempting to take short-cuts, but a life of victory isn't a life without disappointment or hard work.

Listen carefully to wisdom;
set your mind on understanding.
Cry out for wisdom,
and beg for understanding.

PROVERBS 2:2-3 NCV

We can be confident that if God tells us to ask for something,
he wants to grant that request.

To him who is able to do immeasurably more than all
we ask or imagine, according to his power that is at work
within us, to him be glory...for ever and ever! Amen.

EPHESIANS 3:20-21 NIV

God will not fail you when it matters most. He won't even fail you
in the small things. Failure is not possible for God.

I will instruct you and teach you in the way you should go;
I will counsel you with my loving eye on you.

PSALM 32:8 NIV

God is faithful to the deepest needs of your heart;
he knows you full well!

You are the only God to be worshipped,
For there is not a more secure foundation
To build my life upon than you.

PSALM 18:31 TPT

There is much joy and freedom to be found in being who you are.

Cast all your anxiety on him because he cares for you.

1 PETER 5:7 NIV

When God sees you with so much mental and emotional weight,
he wants to give you rest. He can take all of your anxiety
and replace it with peace.

The Lord will be your confidence
and will keep your foot from being caught.

PROVERBS 3:26 ESV

No other person can be you better than you.

I know how to live on almost nothing or with everything.
I have learned the secret of living in every situation,
whether it is with a full stomach or empty, with plenty or little.

PHILIPPIANS 4:12 NLT

Discontentment makes you unhappy and miserable.
It inhibits you from enjoying and embracing every moment of life.

We are what he has made us,
created in Christ Jesus for good works,
which God prepared beforehand to be our way of life.

EPHESIANS 2:10 NRSV

You are God's greatest work of art, created for a wonderful purpose.
He doesn't focus on your flaws; he sees his perfect creation,
and he thinks you are wonderful.

Sketch or attach a photo of a
favorite day at the beach.

Faith is the assurance of things hoped for,
the conviction of things not seen.

HEBREWS 11:1 NASB

In difficult situations, it's your faith that determines the outcome.

To each one of us grace was given
according to the measure of Christ's gift.

EPHESIANS 4:7 NKJV

Sometimes the person in your life that needs the most grace is you.
Love yourself. See yourself the way God sees you.

To all who believed him and accepted him,
he gave the right to become children of God.

JOHN 1:12 NLT

Truly, you are so many things. But above all, you are a child of God.

Your magnificent splendor
And the miracles of your majesty
Are my constant meditation.
Your awe-inspiring acts of power have everyone talking!
And I'm telling people everywhere about your excellent greatness!

PSALM 145:5-6 TPT

God made us to be creative and he wants to inspire our creativity.
That's why he gave us towering mountains, hand painted skies,
starry nights, rippling rivers, amazing wildlife, and the changing of seasons.

Splendor and majesty are before him;
strength and joy are in his dwelling place.

1 CHRONICLES 16:27 NIV

Happiness flees in the midst of tough times,
but joy is there regardless of circumstance.

"Submit to God and be at peace with him;
in this way prosperity will come to you."

JOB 22:21

Like a car that needs to be filled with gas and have the occasional
oil change to operate correctly, your body, mind, and spirit need peace
and rest to operate well.

Whether, then, you eat or drink or whatever you do,
do all to the glory of God.

1 CORINTHIANS 10:31 NASB